CW01337772

TRIUMPH HOUSE
Poetry with a Purpose

HAVING A LAUGH

Edited by

Neil Day

First published in Great Britain in 2000 by
TRIUMPH HOUSE
Remus House,
Coltsfoot Drive,
Peterborough, PE2 9JX
Telephone (01733) 898102

All Rights Reserved

Copyright Contributors 2000

HB ISBN 1 86161 892 1
SB ISBN 1 86161 897 2

FOREWORD

Having A Laugh is a wonderful collection of humorous poetry that contains the 'amusing musings' from a variety of new and established poets. Using their creative talent to full effect, each of the authors tells a funny tale or story to entertain you, the reader.

Subjects vary tremendously from funny poems about family and friends to laughable lines on life in general. Together the writers have created a delightful and enjoyable collection of poetry that you'll return to time and time again.

Neil Day
Editor

CONTENTS

Untitled	Elsie Bateman	1
Designer (C) Rap	Ethel Thomson	2
The Greater Littered Fisher	Sid Hindmarsh	3
The Collection	Val Baker	4
Jam	Gordon Gray	5
Brush Off	John Seddon	6
Transported	Betty Nevell	7
Laughter	Sarah Cain	8
Thinner Fatter Does It Matter	M G Eyre	9
Holidays	Sue Roderick	10
Mutiny	Jan Ollerton	11
Unbottling	Winnifred Edith Ross	12
Naughty Cat	Judith Ruddy	13
Take Care Of Your Teeth	Mary Traynor	14
In Devon	Linda Lawrence	15
Work	Linda Hardy	16
To The College Of Podiatry	Vera Ewers	17
The Gallery Queen: . . .	Jackie J Docherty	18
The Numbers Game	P Sanders	20
Stinky Poo's	D M Turberfield	21
My First Spanish Holiday	E Bourne	22
Our Loo	Hazel Jukes	23
Cooking In The Kitchen	Eva Young	24
I Love You	Claire Bradford	25
Waltzing	Barbara Sowden	26
An Insight Into Parenthood	Michael Anthony Duncan	27
Exercise (Or Exorcise)	Janet Palin	28
Old And Cold	Don Goodwin	29
The Current Position	Andrew M Buchanan	30
Pot Luck!	John L Wright	31
Eric's Nose	Peter Asher	32
A Busy Day?	Patricia Parker	33
Stand To Attention	K Cox	34
Show-Off	Julian Ronay	36
Boney Tony	Tony Emmott	37
Ode To A Giant Bizzie-Lizzie	Betty Glanville	38

Sounds Fishy!	Norman H McGlasham	39
Iggly Dangeroos	J K Booth	40
Untitled	Robert & Christine Appleby	42
Dashing Lady	Frederick Sowden	43
A Glimpse Of The Sun	Lucy Bradley	44
Me Holiday	Sheila Maureen Chester	45
A Place In The Garden	Peggy Wright	46
Ode To A Nurse	Edith Pilkington	48
Despair Before The Affair	Miranda	49
Millennium Man	Elaine Hutchings	50
Building A Bookcase	Babs Bloomfield	51
A Daughter's Laughter	Mary Lawson	52
Substitute?	George Eaton	53
My Hurley Burley Ball	T Robertson	54
May Day	Ray Metcalfe	55
No Teeth	June Williams	56
Ornament	Joanna Carr	57
The Laughter Therapy Farm	Roy Millar	58
Hedgehogs	Mick Nash	60
Boys Can Dance Too!	Kerry Lee	61
Fleas	Susan Woodcock	62
The Pussy Rat	Marie Horridge	63
Night School	Joan Gray	64
Old Bean	John Beals	65
Untitled	Jennie Cranmore	66
Lancashire Fusspot	Eve-Marie Haydock	67
Headless Hector The Noisy Spectre	Norman Ford	68
Get Connected	Anthony Higgins	70
Sore Point	T J Brumby	71
The Sisters	C D G	72
Ring-A-Ding-Ding	Georgina Moore	73
And This Little Piggy	Irene Gunnion	74
Poems	Penelope Moon	75
Mayhem	Anne Rolfe-Brooker	76
Do Not Be Fooled	T C White	77
Bats About Bats	Cate Campbell	78
Good Arrows	Bakewell Burt	79

A Duck's Lament	Hazel Ratcliffe	80
Care Free Is Hair Free	Nick Marsden	81
The Workout	Janette Homer	82
Blue Bolts	P J Littlefield	83
A Woman's Busy Day	Dee Dickens	84
The Perfect Love	Marianne Greenfield	85
The Passion Wagon	Sydney Ward	86
A Rhyme	J M Judd	87
Thought	Tina Watkin	88
Reality	Eira Smith	89
Disrhythmia	Stephen J Holborough	90
The Phone Call	Michael Lee Gooch	91
Little Darling	Ann Stevenson	92
The Brownies	K J Carleton	93
Different Generations' Outings In Southend	Hilary Jill Robson	94
Gut Reaction	Stephen Mason	95
Even Stephen	Francis Arthur Rawlinson	96
The Tail Of A Cat	Lois Burton	97
Time	James Stanley	98
The Springer Spaniel	Frank Ede	99
Ifs, Buts And Maybe	Ivy Cawood	100
Tidy-Up	Samantha McInnes	101
Spin	Rod Trott	102
The Queen Mother's Birthday	Marie Barker	103
Why Me?	Pauline Tattersall	104

Untitled

It finally arrived in the post,
And I went as white as a ghost.
Hubby said, 'Is that the phone bill?
You'd better get me a pill
And then you're in for a roast.'

Elsie Bateman

DESIGNER (C) RAP

Kids today
Got all the gear
Gotta be active
Have no fear
Step out in Reebok
Maybe Dunlop
Boots by Caterpillar
What a thriller
Be a bit sportive
Don the Nike
Ready steady
Time to hike
Don't be a dumbo
Get into Umbro
Go for Puma
Flash the Mizuno
Is it a con
No it's Benetton
Let me guess
Now Ellesse
What the heck
Must be Hi-Tec.

Ethel Thomson

THE GREATER LITTERED FISHER

Vast cloven clay is water-filled and called a fishery,
And stocked with bream and carp and chubb,
Canada geese, swans, mallard clubs
Wagtails, nettles, and docks to rub,
Tormentia, Forget-me-nots, and in green tubes, small trees.

Amid all this, alights and waddles to the water's edge,
A species - Greater Littered Fisher
Bare-buttocked, with a whiskered kisser,
Shell-suited, capped, with baseball visor,
Ground bait is catapulted from its concrete ledge.

Nests in cans, bread wrappers, ranged to ward off all onlookers
It perches on its folding stool
And doesn't move much as a rule
And waves antennae as a tool
To catch fish, throw back, squawk to other hookers.

Leaving the nest for one or two weeks at a time
It food gathers, while wind and rain
Disturbs the cans, and wrappers lain
But on return, when ledge they gain
With flask and smoke and sandwiches, the Fisher adds to them .

Sid Hindmarsh

THE COLLECTION

On the day that we got married
I asked of my other half,
'Could I have some sort of pet?'
'Of course,' he answered with a laugh.
So began the steady collection
Of friends, both feathered and furred,
Until our home resembled a zoo
And dear Hubby thought it was absurd!
He considered the rabbits boring
And the guinea pigs much the same.
He couldn't stand the ferrets -
Oh, he made that very plain!
The dogs he could put up with,
Various cats didn't bother him much;
Though he wouldn't go near the fancy rats
And the snake he wouldn't touch.
There were birds out in the aviary
Lots of fish down in the pond,
A small goat running around the garden
Of which I am rather fond
But then there came the parrot
I suppose that did it in the end
Because she couldn't stand my husband
And only wanted me as her friend.
So he packed up all his belongings
And he left me without a word,
I don't think he was very happy
Being thrown out by a bird!

Val Baker

JAM

Antidisestablishmentarianism
is the second longest word
that I have ever spoken
or that I have ever heard

And yet there is a longer word
or so I've heard it said
That's 'jam' - it's small to start with
but it is inclined to spread.

Gordon Gray

BRUSH OFF

In a little old cottage in the countryside
Was an old fashioned lady, an old fashioned bride.
A man at the door, came to sell his wares
Some interesting gadgets to ease the day's cares
With all purchase details; and a catalogue
Ideal to look through on a trip to the bog.
'I'll have one of those,' she said with a rush.
'Never seen one of those - a *lavatory brush.*'
A month went by and a knock on the door
It's the 'Betterwear' man just as before,
'How are you doing with last month's buy
Did you find it useful? Did you give it a try?'
'It took some getting used to,' she said with a blush,
'But my husband prefers paper, to the lavatory brush.'

John Seddon

TRANSPORTED

I'm longing to see you
But can't raise the fare
So the problem arises:
How to get there?

I *could* come by 'plane
- perhaps walk on the wing -
Or maybe by broomstick -
But it's hardly the thing!

So how about train?
Maybe up on the top?
But it's hard to cling on
And it jolts when you stop!

The coach would be better
But seats must be booked,
And they don't take instalments
- so that idea's spooked!

There's always a car
- But, of course, I don't drive,
And if I hitch-hike
Then I might not arrive!

That leaves horse riding,
Walking, cycling or skates
- But I can't say I'm keen
On the hard work it takes.

So it's back to telepathy
Plus a letter or two
- Though nothing replaces
Close encounters with you!

Betty Nevell

LAUGHTER

There is new illness going round,
For this no cure can be found.
You will get the giggles,
And drop to the floor,
Then wonder if you can take much more.

Your cheeks and sides will start to ache.
You can't stop now,
It's too late.
You're laughing and giggling all over the place
And a huge smile has formed on your face.

You've got the bug,
You've got it bad.
It's laughter you've caught,
And laughter you have.

Sarah Cain (14)

THINNER FATTER DOES IT MATTER

My dearest darling Lynn
Why do you try to stay so thin.
I love you just the way you are
So go on eat that chocolate bar
Don't look at it and try to fight it
Go ahead and you just bite it.
So don't let slimming get to you
Before you know it you'll be ninety-two
And just you think of the pain and sorrow
You may well snuff it today or tomorrow.
I'm not just mocking, I really care
So what we'll do is we shall share.
We'll half the chocolate and the cakes
And see the difference this all makes
If after two weeks this all fails
We'll throw away the bathroom scales
Then we can eat all the chocolate and buns
And between us each weigh twenty tons.
Slimming is a disease which is in your head
So just remember what I said.
You are my gorgeous darling Lynn
The answer is to think thin.

M G Eyre

HOLIDAYS

Holidays? I hate them!
I'm worn out before I go.
With washing, ironing, packing,
Housework and lawns to mow.

I like living on an island.
But hate travelling by plane.
Ships and coaches turn me green
So it's motor car or train.

With the animals in kennels
We indulge in posh hotels.
Abroad we need our passports
And are herded into cells.

It's hard to meet the locals.
Life is so unreal.
We get a taste of native fayre
With every wretched meal.

I loathe living out of cases,
Meeting other people's schedules,
Dressed in freshly purchased clothes
And decked out in evening jewels!

At home I am content
To remain uneducated.
In my opinion Holidays
Are vastly overrated!

Sue Roderick

MUTINY

My husband said, 'Let's get afloat.
It's easy I'll show you the ropes.'
But when he yelled, 'Go aft.'
I heard, 'You're daft.'
So I jumped ship and headed for home.

Jan Ollerton

UNBOTTLING

Now I am not a critic
But I really must complain.
For I can't get at my food
That's supposed to do me good.
With jars that won't unscrew
And packets sealed like glue.
It's impossible for me
To prepare my tea
And when it comes to pain
I struggle all in vain
To undo that cellophane
That will release the pill
And help me feel less ill.
For it's tough enough in life
Without this added strife
And no I'm not a critic
Just an elderly arthritic.

Winnifred Edith Ross

Naughty Cat

Pussy cat, pussy cat where have you been,
in my garden again I've seen.
Your trademark, your calling card dotted around
where you try to hide it in the ground.
I've tried to deter you with different things,
orange peel and bits of string,
to no avail, and then I tried,
plastic bottles with water inside,
windmills rattling round and round,
an army of gnomes, bells ringing out loud,
statues of dogs with eyes that flash,
old tin cans that rattle and clash.
Now I'm stuck for ideas, what can I do
to stop my garden being a loo?
I could hide the soil beneath paved stone,
have a patio there, but then I'd moan,
no flowers or shrubs for my delight,
resigned, I'll just have to give up the fight.
Pussy cat, pussy cat, go elsewhere,
and save me, driven to despair.

Judith Ruddy

TAKE CARE OF YOUR TEETH

Now brush your teeth and keep them clean
Yes, really make them shine
Because I took no heed of this
And now I don't have mine.

Try not to eat too many sweets
They only cause decay
And when you've finished chewing
Just brush the bits away.

Now, when you smile
Your teeth will gleam
And really look quite fine
They look much better in your mouth
Than in a glass like mine!

Mary Traynor

IN DEVON

At nine am each Monday
My class would give their news,
Stories of their weekends,
Soft giggling in the pews.

Small children of just five and six
Full of life and fun,
Young minds alert, inquisitive,
They asked me, 'Where's your mum?'

I said, 'She died some years ago
And now she's up in Heaven,
She's with some friends she used to know,
They played when they were seven.'

A few weeks later 'nine' again
Rosie made a tut,
'Have you some news?' I said to her,
She nodded, eyes full-up.

'On Sunday my dog Muffin
Ran off from my big brother,
Car knocked him down and now he's there
In Devon with your mother!'

Linda Lawrence

WORK

If you need some money you have to go to work -
And see your boss - his face in a smirk.
You smile, but silently call him a berk!
Then stand at a bench with a view of brickwork,
Squashed in with others - some call it teamwork.
At times you ponder about getting outwork,
Which could be fitted in around housework.
But, wouldn't you get richer from doing craftwork?
From your handiwork - artwork, even basketwork?
Earn enough cash from woodwork or glasswork?
Have a go at patchwork, even made a waxwork?
Well, by all means try - but first - Do your homework -
Don't leave it just to guesswork - or -
You might just go -

Berserk!

Linda Hardy

TO THE COLLEGE OF PODIATRY

Many, many thanks from my left and my right
And from the bottom of my feet,
You're just the greatest Foot Patrol
It's been my pleasure to meet.

For fourteen years I've been treated
Since I walked through the great big door
To be led by the hand to the famous chair
And told to, 'Get your feet off the floor.'

The tools of the trade are put to the test,
From toe to heel they give you the best.
I've had corns, hard pad and now fallen arches,
You name it, I've had it, and that's just for starters.

There's a special kind of friendship
That passes between you and me,
It's a cure that's not in a bottle
It's better than a cup of tea.

It's been a pleasure knowing you all
From dear Mr Davis to the John, Kates and Pauls,
To me you're the greatest students
So many names I cannot recall.

It was Kate's idea I should write this poem
After my gaining a special award
From the International Poetry Society
So there you are, that's my final word.

Vera Ewers

THE GALLERY QUEEN:
ONCE YOU GET TO KNOW HER
YOU'LL KNOW WHAT SHE MEANS

'We are the girls of the Old Royale: ever so true and ever so loyal!
From Polka to Can-Can we'll entertain: leaving other Music Halls
                                                                              in the rain.
We've danced at the Palace and the Ritz:
We've kicked high and low and done the splits
We've got some nice treats lined up for you!
You've paid your money and we'll dance on cue!

With a high kick here and a high kick there!
Oh good-natured Charlie we know you're somewhere
When we Can-Can high we're thinking of you!
When we kick low: well you know what you can do!

We've danced topless and nude in the naughty nightclubs in
                                                                                 Paris France
Losing all our young shyness as we give ourselves to total dance
From Paris to London we let the gentlemen enjoy our naked charms
And the good-natured Charlies know they're warm and safe in our arms

I was once a Hot Gin barmaid at the Duchess Dance Hall
Now I know that doesn't sound much to enthral
But just look at the way I now sing and dance
Every night I'm ready and willing for romance.

You may have heard me singing down Knightsbridge way
Especially on a warm and sunny springtime day
For it's twice as nice when the sun beams down
With romance in the air and flowers all around . . .

In for a penny in for a pound!
Anything goes when she's in town
She's the girl that everyone cares for
She's the girl that everyone dares for . . .!

Yes the boys have gambled and lost for me
Oh the boys have fought and died for me
I'm Penny Delightful the Gallery Queen
If you get to know me, you'll know what I mean . . .!'

Jackie J Docherty

THE NUMBERS GAME

All my life new numbers have tumbled through my head,
I was born on the 7th day of June and married 14th Feb.
On the 23rd my daughter was born in the month of May,
And on the 15th August my son will start work on that day.
I need to keep a note of meeting dates and telephones,
My bank account has numbers - so have all my many loans.
I can't keep track as numbers keep buzzing through my head,
I know some day I'll forget my bus or maybe time for bed!
I'm fed up with the need to keep each number in my brain,
I need to count my pennies, watch my weight and still keep sane!
I hope each day there wouldn't be more new numbers to remember,
I can't cope with any more now - is Christmas 12th December?
I'm cracking up quite quickly so that even in my sleep,
I count *each field* they pass through and *each bleat* of those daft sheep
I've decided now to end it all and from this cliff I'll soar,
But still wonder how many feet I'd drop as through the air I fall!
So this is how it all will end - but just one last request,
A cup of tea, a little milk, 3 sugars will taste best.
And when at last they bury me and in the ground I'm laid,
I can see my epitaph in stone - 'He added up - God took away!'

P Sanders

STINKY POO'S

I thought at first 'twas cabbage or, perhaps someone was dead.
Maybe the dog had just blown in; he does when he's not fed.
Then thought perhaps 'twas Grandad, or Grandma sitting there,
Oh Brother! Let me tell you, that stink was pretty rare.

Not the one for complaints, or contrary to most views,
That pong was pretty awful; much worse than stinky poo's.
It stank of rot and decay, of bogs and bodies there.
I tell you this, I had to shift, I'd had my rotten share.

And now to tell the story, to tell what can be said.
You've guessed it right; 'twas not the dog; grandparents or the dead.
'Twas wafting from the gas stove, the oven door ajar;
The cat lay there, all singed, half cooked, across the cooking bar.

Now, how it came to be there, was plain for all to see.
That little moggie, frantic; the same as you or me,
Decided on a bolt hole; In panic, did no wrong.
It did the same as all would do;
Escape that rotten pong!

D M Turberfield

My First Spanish Holiday

I never thought I'd see the day,
Off to Spain, up and away.
A drop of sherry might do the trick
To stop the jitters and feeling sick
But my sister's calm, takes it all in her stride
She often goes just for the ride.
I'm scared of flying so I made my will
I don't want the kids to pay the bill
But if I like it, and enjoy my stay
I might come back another day.
I've packed my case with lots of clothes
And cream to scare of mosquitoes
A little fun and a few days' sun
Could make a difference to this Mum
But I'll soon be back and that's the main
To good old England wind and rain.

E Bourne

OUR LOO

We had some trouble with our loo
And didn't quite know what to do.
We phoned the plumber - round he came
Mended it - then went again.

We thought our troubles there would end
And water flow around the bend.
We pulled the handle - Ray and me
Then both gave up - to have some tea.

Now we've learned just what to do
And pass the good news on to you.
You press the handle - do not rush
Then count to ten.
   'It's a Double Flush!'

Hazel Jukes

COOKING IN THE KITCHEN

I was cooking
In the kitchen,
And cracking an egg,
When it missed the bowl,
And slid down my leg,
It went into my sock
And on to my shoe,
Oh, what a sticky mess
This egg's got me into!

Eva Young

I Love You

I love your eyes
I love your nose
It's big and red just like a rose.

I love your mouth
I love your hair
Its unusual colour is beyond compare.

I love your legs
I love your feet
They're large and flat and smell in the heat.

But most of all I love your figure
Even though it makes others snigger.

Claire Bradford

WALTZING

A young lady who hailed from the city
Set out for the dance looking pretty,
Alas her elastic was weak
Her knickers fell round her feet
And she waltzed on her bum, what a pity.

Barbara Sowden

AN INSIGHT INTO PARENTHOOD

Bloodshot eyes through a sleepless night,
Arguments that will cause a fight,
Gurgles and giggles that bring delight.

Dirty nappies everywhere,
A joy to see and a joy to share,
Fast asleep with loving care.

Eyes and hearts filled with joy,
In their cot with a cuddly toy.

Baby grows and body suits neatly piled,
And this is only the first month of your child.

Michael Anthony Duncan

EXERCISE (OR EXORCISE)
(To free me of an unwanted body)

I'm too small for my weight,
have I left it too late to do anything about it?
Twice a week I go swimming in a pool full of women,
it might help, but I'm starting to doubt it.
If I have my own up, I'm just trying to tone up
what I have to make it feel firm.
And though I feel fitter, I still feel quite bitter,
when I look in the mirror I squirm.
Maybe twice isn't enough to shift flabby stuff,
but I will do some walking as well.
I'll walk all around town to get this weight down,
but it's still not starting to tell.
I've tried shifting the pounds to old rock 'n' roll sounds,
I've tried belly dancing - doesn't suit!
Along with dieting tips I've cut out the chips,
so I'm scoffing the veg and the fruit.
I look at the fashion with a long yearning passion
to be as I was in my teens.
I go and try them on and my hopes are all gone,
as I can't do the zip on these jeans.
So a size 16 I try, as I'm starting to cry
for being an overweight frump.
I'm squeezing in bits, in the hope that it fits,
Oh no! Not another stray bump!
Some day I'll resign myself to my design
and I'll look back on the things I have done.
The exercise and toning, the agony and groaning,
and I'll wonder why keep-fit fans call it fun.

Janet Palin

OLD AND COLD

I wore my socks in the shower because my feet were cold,
It did not really matter because my socks were very old.
My feet were nice and warm, so I decided to wear my vest,
It felt so good that I decided after pondering to wear the rest.
I put my best top coat on, together with my woolly hat,
Then for the next four hours, in the shower I was sat.
My doctor says I'm getting better, I'm not as bad as I used to be,
I no longer have hot water bottles strapped to both my knees.

Don Goodwin

THE CURRENT POSITION

Though the loos in your Show House are sleek,
Can electrical toilets not leak?
Such a shock to see volts
Used to lock or free bolts!
You'll not mind if I don't take a peek?

Each wee room featured here on the plan
In the brochure looks so spick and span
But it's no great relief
If you share my belief
It will all be a flash in the pan.

While your waterless closet just shines
With its towering Ferro designs -
Easy-care nylon floor,
Paper-free pylon core -
I've no urge to purge on power lines!

True, flush fittings, glass and stainless steel
Have a flash, ultra-modern appeal
But the way the bowl zaps
With remote control 'claps'
Makes each 'sitting' a nightmare ordeal.

So design teams have pooled all their brains
To use space-age research to spare drains . . .
If you're done to a crisp
It's no fun when a wisp
Of your bottom line's all that remains!

Andrew M Buchanan

POT LUCK!

Daddy what's a *cannibal* because I want to know,
Darling they were people eaters - that lived long ago.
But Daddy someone told me that they're still around,
In every country in the world, such fiends can be found.
No, they died out long ago when civilisation took a hold,
Like I said before they've all gone, listen to what you're told.
But Daddy surely you are one because you are eating meat,
Daddy why are you sweating so, could it be the sudden heat?
Surely it is relative, like Auntie Flo and them,
We shouldn't eat our families Dad, as that they should condemn.
When you eat those animals Dad, aren't they too flesh and bones?
Come on Dad be honest now, this one learns not moans.
If what you tend to eat is similar with a little take and give,
Then what you have up on your plate Dad must be a *relative!*
Oh dear Dad you are awful, now I want no *ifs* or *buts,*
Stop your cannibalising now Dad and stick to *fruit and nuts!*

John L Wright

ERIC'S NOSE

Eric's nose was one of those
That blotted out the sun
If he turned you had to duck
Or lay down flat, or run.

It was so big, they thought a fig
Was growing there, not hairs -
But when they tried to test the size
The figs dew-dropped like pears

Their clothes were stained
And some complained with a most peculiar gripe -
Their noses grew and the sun turned blue,
For fear of getting swiped.

Peter Asher

A BUSY DAY?

I woke up this morning
And thought to myself
What shall I do today?
The washing, the cleaning, the hovering up
Or maybe I'll phone my friend Kay.
But there's that pile of ironing,
There's shopping to do
And I've got dozens of letters to write.
Then there's the windows
They're so misted up
Who knows if it's daytime or night?
I must visit the dentist
My teeth are on edge,
And my hair looks a terrible sight,
When I've got a minute
I'll get out the steps
And change the dead bulb in the light.
I'll go to the butcher's, the school and the vets
Then pop to the baker's for bread.
I feel so exhausted already - I know
I think I'll spend all day in bed.

Patricia Parker

STAND TO ATTENTION

The National Anthem of Finland is Finnish,
It's easy to end it but hard to beginnish.
The first note's top C, the second's a stumer,
The third one is easy, according to rumour.

Deutschland considers itself 'über alles',
But some of us here think that is all balles.
They lost the World Cup, they lost two world wars,
Their anthem, it seems, is riddled with flaws.

The French sing hurrah for a town in the south,
Its name is not Grimsby and nor is it Louth.
How strange they should pick just one town to extol,
And leave all the others to rock and to roll.

The Spanish, no doubt, sing praises of onions,
And dance funny dances which give 'em all bunions.
They once had a fleet they called the Armada,
Till Drake bowled 'em out - it was on at Grenada.

The Italians eat pasta, which makes 'em sing fasta,
And causes their tower at Pisa to lean.
When Musso, Benito, was high lord and masta,
He dressed them in blackshirts which never were clean.

The United States has a star-spangled banner,
And doughnuts are cheap at eighteen-and-a-tanner.
In Brazil they play football, grow very hard nuts,
In Iceland their kippers don't have any guts.

In Greenland the people are all frozen numb -
You cannot sing well with an ice-cold bum.
In Egypt they have the inscrutable Sphinx,
And the Suez canal full of 'orrible stinks.

In England alone we stay squeaky clean,
And sing like hell to save the Queen.
With rings on her fingers and corns on her toes,
We hope she wins wherever she goes.

K Cox

SHOW-OFF

Look at me
in my expensive ski clothes
twisting and weaving
like a snake
through the powdery snow
what a figure I cut
all eyes
all eyes
are on me
as I skid to a halt
at the end of my run
spraying people with snow
as they sit at their tables
drinking Glühwein
and eating fondue
under the hot alpine sun

but what is happening
I've caught an edge
and I'm falling tumbling
my head in the snow
my feet in the air
the shame of it
and the chalet girls
are laughing
and Hans
the mountain guide
with the piercing blue eyes
is staring

Julian Ronay

Boney Tony

There was a young lawyer called Tone
Whose body was all skin and bone
His gown and his wig
Looked like sacks on a twig
So to falling down grates he was prone!

Tony Emmott

ODE TO A GIANT BIZZIE-LIZZIE

I'm very sorry that I have to say
My Bizzie-Lizzie has had its day.
It happened at the festive season
When we put it outside for a very good reason.
Although I'm sure we were all quite sober
Someone must have knocked Lizzie over
And being so big with branches so thick
She just couldn't move, she felt so sick
We never realized she was so ill
She lay there for days, so stiff and still,
Until I discovered her on the floor
Her lovely flowers they were no more.
We were so upset, we really cried,
For our Bizzie Liz had finally died!

Betty Glanville

SOUNDS FISHY!
Trials and tribulations of fishing

Well, the weather's looking fine,
And we're heading for the Tyne,
For a whole day's fishing on the pier.

To cast your line you cannot wait,
And you've spent three quid on bait,
So if you catch nowt that day can work out dear.

You can stand and stare for hours,
In the gusting wind and showers,
As you contemplate your future and your past.

Your line suddenly goes tight,
And you think 'I've got a bite,'
But that thought just isn't going to last.

On those rocks your hook is snagged,
And that fish you nearly bagged,
Has survived to swim another day.

And oh! lightning and thunder,
There goes another plunder,
Thinks, time to pack the kit away.

So soaked right through and frozen blue,
For home you set to steer,
But are you disillusioned? No,
Next week we'll try the Wear.

Norman H McGlasham

IGGLY DANGEROOS

2.4 in their 4x4 the tribe
went on safari.
The local zoo had much to see
Filling the day for all.

Cheetahs were spotted, penguins, bears,
zebras and others; baby chimps too
out with their mothers.

A day of adventure, fun and
fulfilment with shops to wander,
for gifts and refreshment - with
keepers on guard and keenly observant.

No! came the cry at the time to go
from the youngest of the troupe.
We cannot leave. We cannot leave.
All has not been seen!

The parents scratched and squawked
between them. What was missed? All
sections were seen, all areas tramped.
Still the smallest cried and dancing
feet stamped.

'The Iggly Dangeroos. The Iggly Dangeroos'
was the plaintive wail. No chocolate
could console the cub in distress, only
another trek into the wilderness.

'There, there, there's where they live!'
The finger pointed, expectant and excited.
The big apes looked on, bewildered and
struck dumb. Through the grey bars
amid the hum stared back the notice
of the sub-station.
On a board the legend no longer
incongruous, but clear, bold and plain
to see - Keep Out! Keep Out! *Highly Dangerous!*

J K Booth

Untitled

Asked Camilla, 'Is it true what I hear,
If I kiss you, my prince will appear?'
'If you want Charlie, Miss,
'Twill be more than a kiss!'
Said the frog, with a wink and a leer.

Robert & Christine Appleby

DASHING LADY

There was a young lady from Leek,
Who went to Spain for a week.
There she streaked through town,
Causing senorinas to frown,
But the senors smiled and admired her cheek.

Frederick Sowden

A Glimpse Of The Sun

If the sun shines on a Saturday I wash everything in sight
and create a pile of ironing which lasts 'til Sunday night.
I clean out nooks and crannies, I even scrub the floors,
I seem to spend the whole day cleaning out indoors.

I get pestered by the kids as to things they want to wear
when they know if it's not in the wardrobe - it's hanging up out there.
The telephone always seems to ring when I'm trapped inside a room
having moved most of the furniture to sweep up with the broom.

What is it with these people who won't leave me alone?
If I won't buy it at the door they try and sell it on the phone.
And just as I am thinking my work is nearly done,
somebody, somewhere, goes and nicks the sun!

'Who'd be a mum?' I ask myself when I'm feeling pretty grotty,
I'm covered in wet washing - I'm sure I must be potty.
I plan to murder the weatherman who last night was on my screen,
I'll stick him in a smelly sock in my washing machine.

'There'll be lots of sun tomorrow and no need for complaining.'
He's in a world of his own that man, cos here it's persistently raining!
But then I know it's my own fault, I do get carried away,
All because of a glimpse of the sun on a Saturday.

Lucy Bradley

ME HOLIDAY

Oh the wind it do roar
And the rain it do pour
As I sit in me leaking tent
And I'm peeling me spuds
With me feet in the mud
And me holiday money's spent.
Oh me sleeping bag's wet
And me hair wants a set
And I'm having a lovely time here
And it's doing me good
Like a holiday should
And I won't get no more till next year.

Sheila Maureen Chester

A Place In The Garden

There's this hut - it's our place in the garden
    Father paints each spring of the year
It's shiny and clean, not a smudge to be seen
    Why he bought it was never quite clear.

It commands an elevated position 'mongst grass
    There's wooden steps leading up to the door
There's fancy carved wood 'round roof edges
    Inside there is pink lino covering the floor.

It housed lovely, fluffy angoras
    And they all won prizes galore
Their fur needed hours and hours of grooming
    And they had ten inches of straw on the floor.

The hut took on a fragrance quite 'catching'
    It was sort of earthy, slightly of musk
Reminded me of the days of my childhood
    When the muck cart used to call after dusk.

These furry friends soon went out of favour
    When the neighbour complained of the pong
The kids let loose the bunnies in the gardens
    And ten rows of lettuce - all gone!

Father vowed it was slugs that had eaten 'em
    Or maybe a big army of snails
Everyone knew that Father was fibbing
    Slugs don't have long ears, nor bob tails.

The hut's been well cleaned. An oil drum put in place
 Walls, ceiling and doors painted a delicate blue
Now there's a board nailed to the gate of our garden
 Which reads *'For two pence you can borrow our loo'*.

Peggy Wright

ODE TO A NURSE

A nurse should have written on her back
In words so bright and clear
'Whatever you require, patient
You will find in here'.

She has the backbone of an ox
To lift and carry you
A sense of humour, second to none
To laugh whenever you do.

And feet, they must not be of clay
But light and sprightly ever
So nurse can be at beck and call
And look on it as pleasure.

And sometimes when its *nil by mouth*
And rules she cannot bend
She'll comfort you, and bring to you
A bedpan for your other end.

What would we do without the nurse
The doctors would be lost
Where would we find such service
And at so little cost?

And when you're feeling better
Having got shot of your pain
She'll help you pack your bag for home
And start all o'er again.

She longs to nurse a Richard Gere
Mel Gibson or Tom Cruise, her treat
But when she looks upon his face
It's Fred, from Coronation Street.

Edith Pilkington

DESPAIR BEFORE THE AFFAIR
(dedicated to the master farter)

We are married you and I
But why oh why
Did romance have to fly
Out of the window
Ev'ry time I feel amorous
You fart . . . (you think it's funny now)

What a pity, what a pong
Such a loss
And it's *sooo* wrong
I suffocate
In boredom

All the words you don't say
All the chances you don't take
And you think it's all so safe
But you fart us apart
You break my heart
And you don't seem to care
You slowly blow me
Towards an affair

I need some dancing
I need romancing
I am so sick
Of all your stinking farting

I soon might make my biggest mistake
Cos I have been so gassed of late
I have trouble thinking straight
Now I don't really seem to care
I just desperately need some fresh air

Miranda

MILLENNIUM MAN

What's in a name?
That which is quoth by any other soul can mean much the same
As that which was quilled by the Bard.
Is it really so hard to string words together
To bring one great honour and fame?

Take 'Something is rotten in the state of Denmark' -
Surely not so profound as all that,
Yet remains in the mind, arousing immense admiration.
While 'Summat's up in Oldham' gives rise to no adulation
And is forgotten - just like that.

Even a simple, gentle phrase:
'Soft you now! The fair Ophelia'
Captivates, lingering for days and days,
But 'Shut yer gob, it's that fit-looking wench Doris'
Brings a case of instant amnesia.

Or call to mind that poignant scene; young Hamlet holds a barren
                                              skull aloft -
His tragic cry, 'Alas, poor Yorick! I knew him Horatio',
Brings a lump to the throat and a tear to the eye.
Whereas 'Eh, it's Norman, poor old sod; we were mates y'know, Jack'
Evokes, not a plaintive sigh, but 'Give over; put it back!'

How is it that the words of Shakespeare
Glide off the tongue and alight on the ear
With such ease and plaisir? 'Tis unfathomable;
But still, if you want words which just fit the bill
Look no further than to our inimitable, inestimable, incomparable Will.

Elaine Hutchings

BUILDING A BOOKCASE
(from a flat pack)

We opened the carton with infinite care,
Making sure all of the contents were there.
Five shelves, two sides, a top and a back,
Three fiddly bits and some nails in pack.

A page of instructions in German and Greek,
Italian, French and the one that we speak.
Bobby then laid it all out on the floor,
And nonchalantly said, 'I've done this before.'

I held on to parts which he screwed in place,
He whistled and sang, a smile on his face,
It didn't take long, it was easy as pie,
For Bobby the expert in home DIY.

It looked really grand as it stood by the wall,
Over three feet wide - over six feet tall.
It was firm and straight and upright and true,
But Bobby was glad that he hadn't used glue.

The smile on his face was replaced by a frown,
For the back of the bookcase was on upside down,
The left side was where the right side should be,
So I quickly departed and said, 'I'll make tea.'

Babs Bloomfield

A Daughter's Laughter

Laughter is infectious, they say,
But it all depends on what kind of day you had,
Nothing goes right and when you think it may,
Along comes this lass disguised as a lad.

You don't know whether to be shocked or surprised,
As you stand and stare she returns the glare,
The look of defiance is there,
What can you do to stay aloof?

It is not easy to be civilised,
The air is charged with who knows what!
For a second she looks alarmed,
Then turns on the innocent charm.

Betwixt and between eyes locked together,
Then almost unbelievably,
A spark like lightning appeared,
The mood changed electrically.

Then as if from a great distance,
A rumble of laughter was heard,
Before you knew it seizing the chance,
Joined in the laughter without dread.

You waited for wrath to fall on your head,
You expected her to explode,
But suddenly she smiled a look that said,
I am glad to be your daughter,
As she hugged me tightly,
There was heartfelt laughter.

Mary Lawson

SUBSTITUTE?

My next door neighbour, name of Bill
Said one day 'I'm proper ill,'
So off to London next weekend he went
Now I've never thought of Bill as bent
But three weeks later, back he came
It was clear he was not quite the same
He'd gone off butch, my mate bill
Came back with a bust, name of Jill
The operation had obviously gone well
Now a woman, you just could not tell
I don't mind, I don't really care
But in those tights, all that hair
And down the street in knee-length boot
The cars that slow and give a toot
I wish Bill was back, and all was fine
For I now blush at his washing line
The down side, she now blows a kiss
And says real deep 'Now call me Miss'
I don't judge, not being righteous or holy
But our local team, has lost its goalie.

George Eaton

My Hurley Burley Ball

My hurley burley ball, bounced high above the garden wall.
Then in the breeze, it cleared with ease, the roof and chimney tall
And on the day it soared away, I knew I'd never buy
Another like it, that would hike it, upwards to the sky.
I gave a shout, but without doubt, it ignored my call.

Away it flew into the blue, until it was so small,
No one but me, could even see, that it was there at all.
But it's true, I'm telling you, it's up there very high.
My hurley burley ball.

Watch how you go, for I don't know, when it will start to fall,
But when it does, its dropping buzz, will your ears appal,
And on the ground, circled around, flattened corn will lie.
So where it lands, dig with your hands, then you will maybe spy,
As you fiddle, right in the middle, something round and small.
My hurley burley ball.

T Robertson

MAY DAY

It was a dastardly day on the 1st May
it was raining cats and dogs,
the house roof leaked, my mother freaked
and my sister came round with her scrogs.
The dog was run over, the cat had kittens,
the sewerage backed into the house,
to top it all, my father was mugged
coming home, by a pissed up scouse.
A policeman came to take a statement
but slipped in the s*** on the drive,
he broke his neck as he fell on his head
and he's not expected to survive.
As night-time came the electric went off,
the meter had run out of money,
then to top it all, Aunt Maude arrived
with her cases, it wasn't funny.
'Deary me, did you not get my letter?'
she asked with a sheepish grin,
'I said I was coming, sometime today
to make sure someone would be in.'
'Well it never arrived,' my mother replied,
not in a very good mood,
the last thing she needed right now in the house
was Aunt Maude scoffing all our food.
At last the time came to go to bed
which we all did with some relief,
but at five to two we were all woken up
by another visitor. A bloody thief!

Ray Metcalfe

No Teeth

I know a boy who ate lots of sweets,
He ate them for dinner, he ate them for treats.
He ate them for birthdays, he ate them for trips,
He loved them so much - more than his chips.

One very black day - it came up quite soon,
We couldn't blame it on a phase of the moon,
To the dentist he went - the pain was so great,
The poor boy's face was in a bad state.

The dentist was sad, only one thing to do,
The teeth must come out - it's a shame but it's true,
One quick jab and the boy went out into space,
When he woke up - no teeth - just a big open face.

June Williams

ORNAMENT

I do not think I'm meant to be
A little garden gnome,
This is not my niche in life
I do not feel at home.
There is a crocus at my foot
And several dafferdilly,
With blue tits perched upon my head
I must look bloody silly.
My owner has a Persian cat
So full of charm and grace,
And if I only had the chance
I'd push it in the face.
The ladies say I'm 'too, too sweet'
But now I think of it,
I do not feel 'too sweet' at all,
I feel a proper twit.
The children call me nasty names
Whilst running down the path,
I know that all they want me for
Is just a jolly laugh.
There simply has to be a change
I've made my mind up now,
Tonight I'll really flutter off
And turn into a cow.

Joanna Carr

THE LAUGHTER THERAPY FARM
(You can laugh if you like)

I was taking a break through in Ireland
in the cottage of Jimmy my friend
Jim Daly and I are musicians, to some jigs we were giving a mend
The fiddle and pipes were in great form we stopped for a bit of a craick
The music enlivened our brain cells, imagination we sure didn't lack.

Tea drinking and eating a sandwich, a lump of some nice soda bread
Jim craicked off the unused old barns after we'd watered and fed
We started to blether for pleasure; Jim looked out the window and said
'I could turn these old things into chalets
for tourists to lay down their head.'

At that time the cot had no water, no toilets or lighting at all
An outhouse we used for our functions,
we crapped in an old horse's stall
'I don't think that any tourist would pay for the lack of effects'
'Ah! They'd love the return back to basics,
with nature they could here connect.'

I started to laugh at Jim's theory, he started to laugh back at me
Quite soon we both were in stitches in hysterics with tears in our ee
We could patent a laughter department for tourists to help them unwind
A sign o'er the door,
'you can laugh if you like, it eases the soul and the mind'.

There'd be treatment of varied descriptions each as accord to your need
For belly laughs, belly laugh barns and belly laugh there till you deid
If you wanted a bit of a snigger at something that somebody said
Your privacy would be respected, to the snigger shed you would be led.

If you wanted a schoolboy-like chortle, Billy Bunter is your type of fun
We feed you as well, you can laugh as you eat,
your prescription - a chortle-type bun
Perhaps you're a tired old earl, and need a wee lift in your life
You can guffaw with zest in a garret
and expunge your old bones of their strife.

As we laughed at our improvisation, Jim was inspired and thought
John MacLaughlin is coming tomorrow,
a brand new daft hat he has bought
We could hire him to walk round the farm
giving mirth to our glum clientele
He could be our own clown, no need to dress up,
all he does is just be himsell.

So ended our tea and craication, we returned back again to the jigs
Next morning the day was so lovely, the sun it spilled over green rigs
Each day in your life can be different, the weather be foul or fair
You can leaven your bread with humour and jest
and lighten your soul from its care.

Roy Millar

HEDGEHOGS

There must be several different kinds of hedgehogs,
I saw one in a book the other day,
He looked just like a guinea pig with prickles,
With little legs to help him run away.

Perhaps that's how they breed them in the country,
Maybe the country air and all that green
Enables them to grow like little footballs,
And not a bit like all the ones I've seen.

The ones I've seen are two feet in diameter,
And round about a centimetre high,
And they don't run around on little leggies,
They just lie in the road! I wonder why?

Mick Nash

BOYS CAN DANCE TOO!

The boys in his class called him names
But he had more stamina when it came to games.
They teased and sneered for what seemed an age
Until they saw him on the local stage.

His dancing showed style and athletic grace
He moved over the boards at a tremendous pace.
His jumps left his comrades with mouths open wide
When he did the splits they nearly cried!

He completed each dance with charm and ease
Then sat with a beautiful girl upon his knees.
So now his ballet school has four new lads
There's Fred and Bill - and both of their dads!

Kerry Lee

FLEAS

I think my cat's got fleas
I can tell, he scratches and bites
These dreadful fleas bring him to his knees!

He looks so graceful as he strikes a pose
But not so graceful when a flea is crawling on his nose!

A flea collar around his neck he wears
But he gets his front leg stuck
And he walks around like an animal in a snare
So this collar I think I will have to chuck.

I've put flea powder on him
Until he's covered
To tell the truth, I don't think he's bothered.

No even I escape the flea
I am bit on my ankle, foot and knee
This clever flea's not so dumb
He's even bit me on my bum!

Susan Woodcock

THE PUSSY RAT

When I was only three years old
One bright and sunny day
I made Grandad's blood run cold
In the garden where I played.

It darted here, it darted there
I wondered what was that
Then it jumped into the air
Was that a pussy cat?

I caught it and I held it tight
I would not let it go
It gave Grandad a big fright
He said 'Drop it' - I said 'No.'

He cried 'That's not a pussy cat
Please listen to what I say
You are cuddling a filthy rat
Now let it run away.'

I got scrubbed from head to toe
My skin was red and sore
And I never wanted pussy rats
To play with anymore.

Marie Horridge

NIGHT SCHOOL

Enrol at night school and learn something new!
But what? is the question, what shall I do?
Shall I learn operatics, or dance, do PE?
Or look for the branches of my family tree?
Shall I fathom the mysteries that make my car run?
Or cook with wholefoods and bake a new bun?
Shall I learn a new language, or to sail on dry land?
Try computing or typing or even shorthand?
Keep fit, pop mobility, and now there is swing
For old and for young they're the very *in* thing!
There are so many choices, my head's in a spin,
Think I'll pick up my knitting and stay right in!

Joan Gray

OLD BEAN

On my land I plant a bean
  An old bean I found in the washing machine
    It will grow if it is keen
      They say runner beans help to keep you lean
        In the field my sole bean grows
          Pods appear for which I give a cheer
            Now full of beans I feel fine
              I cut the plant down it's past its prime
                My old bean is now a has been
                  And I'm fat not lean, I beam.

John Beals

UNTITLED

There was a young lady from Lancing,
Who was heavily into line dancing,
She discarded her bra,
And they said, 'Oh, la, la,'
Delighted to see her boobs prancing.

Jennie Cranmore

LANCASHIRE FUSSPOT

'Morning love - what's it today?'
She casts her eyes about the trays.
She looks at the bacon, orders some steak,
I'm wrapping it up when she says, 'Oh, wait!
It's not lean enough. I can't eat fat.
I'm sorry chuck, but it'll have to go back.'
'That's alright,' I say through gritted teeth
and lead the old hag with my fork to the beef.
'It's for me 'usband y'know. He's like a big baby.
Eeh - d'you know? Go on, serve the next lady.'
I serve the next lady and three others more
and still the old woman's no nearer the door.
I take in her appearance but try not to stare,
the wrinkles and blue rinse; the mole sprouting hair.
Weaving tracks up her legs are varicose veins,
her outsize dress sports old gravy stains.
'If it's not any bother, could you just weight me out
one or two sausage, coz it's better than nowt.'
So far I have given her my undivided attention
and so I feel that it's time to make some helpful suggestions.
'How about a nice half shoulder of lamb?
And a breast or a fillet would do any man.'
From counter to counter the old woman follows,
then says, 'No I'll leave it, but I'll see you tomorrow.'

__Eve-Marie Haydock__

HEADLESS HECTOR THE NOISY SPECTRE

Hallowe'en! And I fear mad Sir Hector
Has been walking the West Wing again,
For last night I heard moans and the creaking of bones,
And the ominous rattling of chain.

He's turned up each year since they topped him,
At the spot where his victims were slaughtered,
It must be quite daunting to contemplate haunting
When once you've been hung, drawn and quartered.

But they must have refitted his entrails
For the task for which Hector was fated,
And one has to admit, he's surprisingly fit,
For a man from his head separated.

The vicar prescribed exorcism,
As the way noisy ghosts could be grounded,
But the cleansing routine just made Hector more keen,
To judge by the way that he sounded.

I've tried guard-dogs and man-traps and mothballs,
Made up balms for his aches and his pains,
I've renewed rusty locks and I've knitted him socks,
Bought some Castrol for oiling his chains.

Kept awake by his shrill lamentations,
I sought out the finest throat tonic,
And I hired a man from La Scala, Milan,
To make Hector's voice more harmonic.

But nothing, it seems, could deter him
From these spectral cacophonous jaunts.
So, I've just called to say that I'm going away
Till I hear it's close season for haunts.

Norman Ford

GET CONNECTED

A plug is a plug
Being stuck in snug
Into a small pocket
Flat wall socket
Cutting shape rather small
Wires three in all
Blue, brown, yellow/green
Glasses on to be seen
Twist into right channel
Connect to separate panel
Screw down tight
Push and shove to fight
Each wire to its connection
Done to perfection
Place the back on
Wasted wire gone
If it's all done right
Into socket same height
Now is the time
Press switch on line
Hopefully, now all go
Easy don't you know.

Anthony Higgins

Sore Point

When there's powdering to be done
It's hard to reach some places
Difficult it is for some
Pulling hurtful faces

Trying to reach the chosen spot
Stretching fit to bust
Don't want powdering to clot
Just a sprinkling of dust

It's a very practised art
Can't be learned too soon
Else the powder thus will dart
All across the room

So I send a little puff
If you'll excuse the phrase
To help you reach, when in the buff
That awkward little place

T J Brumby

THE SISTERS

Susan, Myra, Sarah and Pam also Rachel too,
These are the sisters who really like to do,
Most things . . . so crazy . . . you would not believe,
They are all so special, that's easy to perceive.
They all help each other, whenever things go wrong,
Just like sisters should . . . they all get along.
If you get to know them well and treat them all the same,
You will have a special night . . . they're not very tame!
Going out on birthdays and on special nights,
Some wearing stockings and some wearing tights.
The sisters are so full of joy and not of any fright,
Some wearing knickers and some of them might?
After a good night, it's time to get some eats,
Let's find a Chinese take-away and look at all the treats.
After all that dancing, you'll need to get some rest,
So I think it's home for me, I think I've stood the test!
The sisters are so special, they live life with such zest,
Do treat them all alike, they all deserve the *best!*

C D G

Ring-A-Ding-Ding

There was a young Scot from Argyll,
Who wore his Highland dress with style,
When asked with a lilt,
'What's under your kilt?'
'My mobile' he replied with a smile.

Georgina Moore

AND THIS LITTLE PIGGY

A classic beauty there
I smooch your snout
Little piggy friend
What's you all about?
Camera shy
Chance full of mirth
In your 'bulky bacon'
Rollin' girth
Sweet grizzle chin
How a heart doth bleat
So sad I am
Some see you
To eat.

Irene Gunnion

POEMS

Oh may I write a poem for you
That scans and rhymes with metre too
The likelihood is very weak
The poet in me hard to seek
Instead I'll write a silly hum
To start my brain I'll scratch my tum
So here we go - you're ready now?
Look seriously with furrowed brow.

Water dripping, sunshine shafts
Fairy ropes 'a joke' he laughs
What a joy this magic place
A smile of peace upon my face
Up there the water hurtles fast
Foaming suds go floating past
Down here it's still and dusty too
Petals and leaves go bobbing through.

Well that's enough of scan and metre
I'd rather write a poem to Peter
It's such a shame that he's called David
I wonder if my rhyme he's savoured?
And David doesn't rhyme with metre
I'll change his name it's so much neater
Now that's enough so off I go

A poem? Answer 'yes' or 'no'.

Penelope Moon

Mayhem

I could not find the Cuckoos in the parlour
And the Thrushes on the shelf were very few.
I swept the little Sparrows from the bookcase,
And put the massive Barn Owl out on view.

I rounded up the Swallows in the bedroom,
And put them with the Pheasants in the hall.
I had some bother with the Leghorn Chickens -
I could not find the bloody things at all!

The Crows were cawing wildly in the kitchen,
As I put the Mallards in the sunken bath.
I fell across a Starling in the garden
As I drove the twenty Goslings up the path.

I couldn't find the Cockatiels you sent me,
And I fear now that I never will.
I couldn't count the Pigeons on the garage,
But I saw a flock of Blue Tits on the sill.

The Rooks seem very happy in the pantry,
And the Chaffinches are getting very fat.
I'll just round up the Robins in the guest room,
And then I guess I'll go and feed the cat . . .

Anne Rolfe-Brooker

DO NOT BE FOOLED

I wonder if ever
When you read a clever
Poetic endeavour
You stop for a time,
To ponder the notion
That paired, say, the ocean,
With Austrian groschen,
In order to rhyme?

Or what inspiration
Matched confabulation
With triangulation
Implying, of course,
How clever the poet is
To rhyme thus and know it is
Sufficient to show it is
A true tour de force?

But verbal dexterity,
And shameless temerity,
Will reap from posterity
No praises benign.
The true cognoscenti,
With reasons aplenty,
Will soon recognise
That, beneath the disguise,
There dwells no virtuoso,
But rank Mafioso.
Some Tom, Dick or Harry,
Whose skill is to carry
A rhyme dictionary -
Exactly like mine!!!

T C White

BATS ABOUT BATS

Softly through the night you fly
Only stillness passes by
Over hill and over vale
Glinting past the moon so pale
Little wings brush the air
Sonic beams show you're there
Silence shattered by your squeak
As your midnight snack you seek.
Twinkle, twinkle little bat
How I wonder what you're at
Fleeing through the sky so high
No one sees you passing by
Little children how you scare
As to swoop, you prepare.
Stories told both old and new
Of battles fought and dangers slew
Furry mouse flying strong
To fly with you oh how I long
To skim the dark without a care
I see, I hear, but don't know where?

Cate Campbell

Good Arrows

The first game on the dart board,
We ever did play,
Was down at 'the local',
One rainy day.

The board on the wall,
Looked so big and so round,
But when the first dart was thrown,
There came a 'tinkling' sound,
A light that once had lit up the board,
Now formed 'a jigsaw' laid out on the floor.

With a replacement provided,
We tried once again,
To aim for treble-top, but got the hole in the ten,
We agreed that with doubles,
We'd better leave them for a year,
And only attempt them if the pub was all clear.

As for the first time we aimed,
For that dreaded 'double-one',
All the darts - they bounced out,
And 'called time' on the gong.

Bakewell Burt

A Duck's Lament

I'm just a little duck
But I haven't had much luck,
I just opened me beak for dinner
And now I'm getting thinner
'Cos the thing that I just swallowed
Was a fish hook sharply followed
By a float all bright and shiny,
And now me throat so tiny
Hurts, how it hurts.

So you fishermen spare a thought
Next time some fish you've caught,
It's us ducks and swans who suffers
When you act like thoughtless buffers.
Keep your tackle in your baskets
Then we won't need no caskets.

Hazel Ratcliffe

CARE FREE IS HAIR FREE

Once upon a time
There was a princess friend of mine.
Arranged in finest tangerine
Her robes gave off a wondrous sheen.
Yet still her life was incomplete
Her sorrow she could not defeat
For, though she had a beauteous dress
Her hair, it was a ghastly mess.

So messy was indeed her hair
All from far and near stopped to stare.
To stare at curls which had no end -
Or beginning and they could comprehend.
The strands like brambles grew so fast
That, like a flag upon a mast
They stood out for all to see
Stretching from here to eternity.

None could tame her unruly locks
Their scissors broke like ships on rocks.
Rocks which defied all human hands
From barbers skilled throughout the lands.
Her hair became a tangled thread
Through which none would dare to tread.
Birds descended to build their nests
Then came locusts and other pests.

One day the princess caught a chill
And sensing death she made a will
With the princess' final breath
These words she spoke before her death:
*'Cut down the branches and the twigs
And use my hair to make your wigs!'*

Nick Marsden

The Workout

I joined a gym 'cos I was fat
To trim, to tone, to tan and all that
I climbed the stairs and looked around
This is my plight and what I found
The women there were red of face
Glenys, the coach was on their case
Room for one more, come on in
My one-minute circuits about to begin
I pushed, I pulsed, I stretched, I sweat
I lunged, I lifted, repetitive you bet
She swung the stop watch in the air
Come along ladies you know I care
Let's have that bit of extra pull
Smile please, now don't look dull
Just persevere and think of me
Remember to finish off with CV
Just regard me as your nemesis
Who's come to train you all at Genesis
Some pay millions for one to one
But they're not having as much fun
We work your mind, your body and your face
Equip you to fluidly move with grace
When the pounds and inches slip away
You'll think of Glenys and make her day.

Written by a Glenys Groupie.

Janette Homer

BLUE BOLTS

I like the wind in my hair, and clean clothes to wear,
Love reading and writing, and movie star sighting,
Walking for miles, a night on the tiles,
A pint at the club and a soak in the tub,
Flowers in spring and White Christmas by Bing,
Anything from ancient China or Peru, surprises, shocks and bolts
                                                  from the blue,
Castles in Spain and the sweet cooling rain,
Painting the wall and kicking the ball,
Running the team, is my ultimate dream,
Watching the web and its spider, the innocent fly who becomes the
                                                  mealtime provider,
Odd shaped glass jars, through my telescope watching Venus and Mars,
The setting sun across the bay, and what the philosophers have to say,
Jimmy Nail's 'Crocodile Shoes' and Tommy Steele's 'Singing
                                                  The Blues',
Wheeling and dealing and painting the ceiling,
Losing and winning after I'd set the wheel spinning,
Sunday morning's hush, before humanity's rush,
I love belts and braces and a day at the races,
Knick-knacks and oddities and foreign commodities,
I like bric-a-brac and bells and strange but true tales,
I'd adore a Maserti in black and a curtain for the track,
Hotpots and shepherds pie bring a twinkle to my eye,
Churches and tombs and uncluttered rooms,
There is something appealing about that old loving feeling,
'The Last Post' and 'Abide With Me' reduce me to tears as does
                                          'For Those In Peril On The Sea',
I love cup losers and winners, all saints and sinners,
Climbing the stairs without any cares,
Sleeping till nine, and the calling of time,
Children who sing 'We Want William For King',
A spud in its jacket not mash from a packet,
But the thing I love most is Marmite on toast.

P J Littlefield

A Woman's Busy Day

I am a woman small and thin,
Putting rubbish in a bin,
I'm always rushing all the time,
Do all my chores that I can find,
But never find the time to rest,
Even though I try my best,
I'm rushing, rushing round and round,
And then I have to go to town,
Get the shopping, get the bus,
Now it's time for home so rush,
Do the dinner, children home,
Oh what a day I'm nearly done,
Now's the time to get a cuppa,
Oh my god it's time for supper,
Do the supper, go to bed,
So I can rest my weary head.

Dee Dickens

THE PERFECT LOVE

'I love you' he says
With so much feeling,
'I love you' he says
With no wheeling or dealing.

'I love you' he says
With that quizzical look,
That's as easy to read
As my favourite book.

No tantrums, no sulks,
He knows how things stand.
He knows there's another,
I'm wearing his band.

'I love you' he says
As I turn, to depart.
Knowing he's the *one* parrot
That's captured my heart.

Marianne Greenfield

THE PASSION WAGON

Maureen and Doug had everything in order,
The day they set out and went over the border.
A van they were after and a van they did buy,
And back over the border the pair they did fly.

This van it was special as a Merc was its make,
Its colour is white and a big load it can take.
Now the pair had in mind this vehicle they'd fashion,
To change from a van into a wagon of passion.

So into this wagon our Doug set to labour,
There were things that he fitted that were in Maureen's favour.
A wardrobe and kitchen, a loo and a bed,
And even on the floor some lino was laid.

There is carpet and curtains and tie-backs as well,
Our Doug thought of everything, to be in it you could tell.
So Maureen shouts Doug drop all and let's go,
Just get those wheels rolling, it's time didn't you know.

And so let me tell you if this wagon you see,
On the roads as you journey it'll be Maureen and Doug-ie.
They'll be heading for somewhere to park for the night,
With their heads on the pillow, they'll cuddle up tight.

And as you would read this with passion in mind,
Just think of our couple leaving everything behind.
They're travelling around in their wagon of passion,
As if everything else has gone out of fashion.

And as I would close now with the white Merc in mind,
I'm sure you'd agree with me it was certainly a great find.
For Maureen and Dougie, life will ne'er be the same,
As it was in their passion wagon, they learnt many a game.

Sydney Ward

A Rhyme

I've tried to write some words,
That fall in the right places.
And think of things for in-between,
To fill in all the spaces.

To write in fact some lines that rhyme,
Now that is quite a feat.
One word, then two, and before you know
Your verse is so complete.

It's not so easy writing rhymes,
Making it all sound right.
And sometimes getting muddled up,
And forgetting what you're doing! 'See.'

I've done the very best I can,
And wrote it line for line.
I think I've wrote a poem
And even made it rhyme.

J M Judd

THOUGHT

There's only one thing wrong
with being a poet
that's rumbling round
in my head.

I shall have to get
plenty of stuff written down
to be famous,
when I'm *dead.*

Tina Watkin

REALITY

Such a pretty picture we see at Christmas time.
The cards with stars and snowflakes - so prettily they rhyme.
But Christmas morn for Jesus was dirty, cold and dark,
A cattle shed with straw and hay - a manger cold and stark.
No nice warm cot and blankets - no doctor standing by.
And yet this baby - Son of God - was sent for us to die
God wanted us to know his love, so sent His only Son
To live among the people until their hearts He'd won.
He worked and walked among them and shared their joy and pain,
So that He can identify with all our loss or gain.
He understands our suffering, He understands our tears,
You see He felt it all before, the joy, the hurt, the fears.
He suffered death on our behalf and knew rejection too,
Yes each and all emotions He went through just for *you*.
But now He's with the Father and hears each plea and prayer,
He'll answer us with loving heart and all our lives He'll share.
We only have to kneel and pray and ask forgiveness too,
He's waiting now to change our lives so we can start anew.

Eira Smith

DISRHYTHMIA

'Last train's gone,' the porter said. 'Don't know when the next will be.'
So here we are stranded together - Disrhythmia and me.
The fire burned low in the waiting room, its embers dying out in
                                                      the hearth
Now just a glow getting dimmer in the place it had blazed at its birth.
I turned up my collar to keep out the cold and tried to settle down
But as as restless as the wind outside, now blowing the darkness around
Rearranging day with night in slow subtle shades of grey
The telegraph wires sang Disrhythmia, and serenade specially for me.
Before me stretched an endless night, time to think at last
And spend it all in silent violence squeezing out the past.
Just me and Disrhythmia and a romantic little scene
Stranded in a railway station dining from the chocolate machine.
So through the night I passed the time in the railway station hall
Engrossed within the past that was the posters on the wall
A thin brown film of cigarette filth had stained them a hue of sepia
The words they had all been removed their replacements read
Disrhythmia.
I smiled and thought of the doctor when he turned and looked away
'It seems you have Disrhythmia' - what more is there to say?
I heard a train approaching, but made no move to be
Its passenger as through it steamed and screamed a loud
                                                       Disrhythmia at me.
Around me swirled a steam, coal mist of damp and warming grime
As it cleared the station board appeared cracked and broken down
Its jumbled letters spread about became visible to me
Disrhythmia.
I see.

Stephen J Holborough

THE PHONE CALL

Ring! Ring! 'Coming' I shout
Ring ring! 'In a minute' I say
Ring ring! 'Hold your horses' I yelled just the other day
Ring ring ring! 'Right that's it' I growl as I pick up the phone
'Hello, hello!' I say in my usual cheerful way.
'Who's there?' I asked 'Who's there?'
But no-one answers my questions or gives me a simple reply
and the phone line goes completely dead as if someone's screwing
with my head, so I mutter something rude, then hang up the line at my
end, don't you just hate those prank callers
because they drive me around the bend!

Ring, ring, ring, ring, *ring, ring!*
Oh here I go again, so I pick up my receiver
thinking it might happen again.
But it's just an old friend from Surrey
who had a bad connection, at the other end.
We talked for hours and hours
I thought we'd never end
Isn't it nice, when you get a phone call
From one of your closest and dearest
friends!

Michael Lee Gooch

LITTLE DARLING

Sticky fingers on the glass
Chairs and cough all full of grass.
Shoes and socks strewn on the floor
Chocolate streaks all down the door.

Telly Tubbies on the tape
Faces all covered in creamy cake.
Smiles and tears, and little tantrums
Such are the joys, shared by Grandmas.

Though, secretly they just love it
As, with relief, at five o'clock,
Parents arrive to collect their tots.
So with a sigh, and a well-earned rest,
Are ready again, for tomorrow's test

Of patience, love and endurance;
For the tiny tots
Who comes to rule us!

Ann Stevenson

THE BROWNIES

There's a brown owl, sitting by me,
with large brown eyes, wild and free.
in the yard beyond, a brown dog yaps,
at a little brown hen, and two brown cats,
the two brown cats, spotted a brown bird,
his presence, no more was heard.
Saved, was the brown mouse, while the brown
cats were occupied, then my eyes returned, to
the wise brown owl, with the large brown eyes,
sitting by me, wild and free, and I mused to
myself, this must be the 'Brownies'!

K J Carleton

DIFFERENT GENERATIONS' OUTINGS IN SOUTHEND

No such 'fings' as 'olidays for likes of us
Once-a-year Beano on a 'chara' bus,
Went 'wiv' the lads; bunch of scallywags,
'Fought' we 'woz' 'cat's whiskers' wearing our 'glad rags'!
Loaded bus 'wiv' beer crates running at gallop,
The boys liked a 'skinful' of favoured 'wallop'!
Pal pocketed 'mouf'-organ for a sing-song,
Not unknown for two mates to 'ave punch-up, ding-dong,
A scrap over 'nuffink', 'boff' ending up 'wiv' 'shiners,
Tough as they 'woz', afraid to face 'old chinas'!

Sons; past draping knotted 'ankies on their 'eads,
Or turned-up 'trowsies' to paddle beach beds,
Arrive in cars each with family,
Bring swimming gear, play beach ball if chilly,
Enter aquarium and 'venture playground,
Catch pier train to see show and view coast around,
Visit watersports centre facilities,
Hire surfboards to ride until splashdown canopies,
First generation's finale 'knees-up muvver' Brown,
Son's drive home wearied from lively Southend town.

Hilary Jill Robson

Gut Reaction

My belly was a shy smile that hid from cameras and women like you.
Not so much a six-pack, as a back pack on the front.
My old zip-less cardigan that used to keep me warm.
A pillow stuffed with jam and cheese and milk.
My bald school friend to whom I'd confide.
Who never lied.
An inverted bath tub always full, fun and gurgling.
My cuddly love bundle rotunda,
My ticklish Welsh-white tundra.
Hanging like a landslide,
Laughing like an earthquake
Breaking icy silence.
As warm as your breath.
As soft as your lips.

Stephen Mason

EVEN STEPHEN

Even Stephen pizza kebab
Stephen was a very bad lad
When the policeman asked his name
The one he gave was not the same

Not a word would pass his lips
Until he had ate his burger and chips
Then he sat down and cried
Feeling sorry because he had lied

Francis Arthur Rawlinson

THE TAIL OF A CAT

Hector was a tom cat, a common breed was he.
He'd never had a pedigree, or anything like that.
His home was an alley, on the seamy side of town
His coat was sort of brown, white beneath his tummy.

Hector he was growing old, his prime of life was done,
When danger loomed, he could not run, nights getting cold.
He decided to move away, to a retirement home, somewhere,
He said a prayer, 'Please find me a place today.'

He passed the town, went up the hill,
To where the rich folk dwelt. He passed the green belt
Alongside the water mill.
The gentry set dogs on him, kids pelted him with stones,
Parlour maids met him with groans, his prospects looked grim.

He continued to walk on, dejected, weary and worn,
Began to wish he'd never been born, his hopes seemed gone.
Then he saw a cottage nestling in the wynd, honey brown stone, thatched roof,
A neat garden, proof that the folks were kind.

He slipped under the gate, limped towards the door,
A voice said 'You look poor, come and rest your pate,'
Now wintry storms do blast, and shake the briars,
Snug before a blazing fire, Hector purrs 'I'm home at last.'

Lois Burton

TIME

Time is like a bucket of water
with a hole in the bottom.
In the beginning, there is so much water
it is hard to imagine that the bucket
will ever run dry,
but as the water level gets nearer
to the bottom of the bucket,
we begin to think about
whether we have used the water wisely,
or just allowed it to drain away.

James Stanley

The Springer Spaniel

He wakes me each morning, quite softly, not loud
He walks me each morning and holds his head proud.
He knows when I'm down, he knows when I'm up
He brightens my day and he filleth my cup.

Every sound he will know that is made in the house,
When he likes he can be as quiet as a mouse.
A knock on the door and he'll bark and he'll bay,
No one comes in till he's checked they're okay.

Meal time's the second best time of the day
His appetite's large but his manners 'parfait'.
He never refuses, he'll eat what you wish
And when he has finished he'll bring back his dish.

When he's out in the field he reigneth supreme
No Labrador goes where he has been.
Thick bramble and nettles cause him no concern
Just watch, it's surprising just what you will learn.

Evenings he may when we lounge after tea
Either lay by the fire or against the settee.
Should anyone move he'll make for the door
He stands on three legs and he raises a paw.

If it's safe to go out when he's been on patrol
And there's nobody loitering, not even a mole
He'll ask for his bed to be put by the door
It's sleep-byes time and he's on guard once more.

So during the night nothing moves but he knows,
Even the beds creak, when we wriggle our toes.
Guard dog or gundog he's quite a humdinger
There's only one spaniel for me, that's a *springer*.

Frank Ede

IFS, BUTS AND MAYBE

If only I had lots of cash,
I think that I would make a dash
For pastures new, and see the world,
If only I'd some cash . . .

But that's a dream, and ain't my scene,
I've never had much money.
But if I had . . . then I'd be off
To a land of milk and honey.

Well, maybe if I slave and save?
Then I'd be in a rut!
If only I'd some cash to wave: . . .
Instead of ifs and buts . . .

Ivy Cawood

TIDY-UP

T idy up always
I n every corner
D on't put it off
Y ou'll regret it.

U ntil you tidy up
P lease don't come to my house.

Samantha McInnes

SPIN

Tony: Are we spinning yet?
Doctor: Oh yeah!
Today we're spinning like a top
Like kids around a candy shop
The media's beating down the door
To hear the spin they heard before
It's the same old, same old warmed up dream
Just a variation on a theme
A little bit of slight of hand
The fools will never understand
Oh yes! My friend we're spinning well
And the truth is going straight to hell
The lies are neither here nor there
So smile that smile as if you care
And give them sun and give them shine
And watch me spin another line
Then pray they think that I'm sincere
So we can spin another year
Tony: Are we spinning yet?
Doctor: Oh yeah!
You bet!

Rod Trott

THE QUEEN MOTHER'S BIRTHDAY

The Queen Mother has reached 100
She is so firm footed!

Alec Stewart has made 100 runs
And also it's his 100th match!

What is their secret of their strength?
Do they exercise? How, why and when?

Let us into the secret
Then we will be fit!

Marie Barker

WHY ME?

A little fly sat down one day
   and asked himself 'Why me?
Why don't I have the colours
   of a vibrant honey bee?
Why can't I have the lustrous wings
   of a graceful butterfly
That shimmer in the midday sun
   as he gently flutters by?

I could have been a ladybird
   with a coat of red and black
And settle on the greenest leaves
   to have my daily snack,
A dragonfly I'd love to be
   with two pairs of slender wings
And glide along so skilfully
   on rivers, ponds and streams.

And if I was a songbird
   a nightingale or thrush
I'd warble out the sweetest trill
   from daybreak until dusk,
The swiftness of an eagle
   soaring high up in the sky
Over mountains, dales and valleys
   oh, 'Why a fly - oh why?'

And as the little fly took stock
   on what seemed so unfair
He looked up just in time to see
   a hand raised in the air,
One of those humans yet again
   his enemy number one
'Why me?' The little fly exclaimed
   then the little fly was gone.

Pauline Tattersall

INFORMATION

We hope you have enjoyed reading this book - and that you will continue to enjoy it in the coming years.

If you like reading and writing poetry drop us a line, or give us a call, and we'll send you a free information pack.

Write to :-
**Triumph House Information
Remus House
Coltsfoot Drive
Peterborough
PE2 9JX
(01733) 898102**